MICHAEL BERENSTAIN'S

RAPTOR ATTACK!

illustrated by **Jesse Clay**

GT
PUBLISHING
New York

The *Tyrannosaurus rex* and other meat-eating dinosaurs of long ago were huge and fierce and strong. But were they the most ferocious dinosaurs of all? Probably not!

The most ferocious of all the meat-eating dinosaurs may have been the raptors— *Velociraptor* and its relatives.

Ve-lo-ci-<u>rap</u>-tor

The raptors were not very big.
The *Velociraptor* was only six feet long
and not as tall as a man.
But, it had a very big appetite!

The *Velociraptor* had jaws full of sharp teeth.

Its hand-like fore feet had long claws.

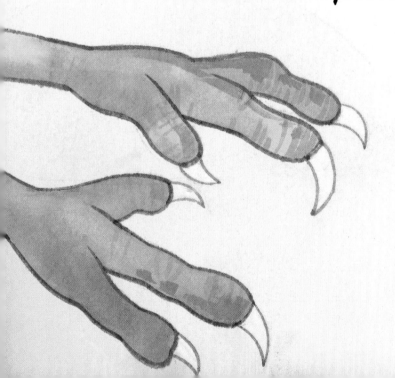

And each of its hind feet had one very big,
curved claw.

The *Velociraptor* was fast!
It chased after and caught its prey.

The *Velociraptor* held up its big rear claw when it ran. But when it attacked, the *Velociraptor* pulled that big curved claw down like a cat stretching out its claws.

The *Velociraptor*'s tail was very stiff and strong.
This helped it keep its balance when running fast.

The *Velociraptor* may have hunted in packs like wolves, chasing and attacking much larger dinosaurs. Perhaps the *Velociraptor's* prey included the *Tenontosaurus*, a medium-sized relative of the duck-billed dinosaurs. Fossil bones of some of these plant-eating dinosaurs have been found near those of some *Velociraptors*.

Ten-<u>on</u>-to-saur-us

The *Velociraptor* may also have raided the nests of other dinosaurs to eat their eggs and young.

The skeleton of a *Velociraptor* was found clutching the skull of a *Protoceratops* as though the two had killed each other in a fight. Some *Protoceratops'* nests were found in that area.

Had the *Protoceratops* died defending its nest?

Pro-to-<u>ser</u>-a-tops

The *Velociraptor* was part of a family of dinosaurs called dromaeosaurs (dro-<u>mee</u>-o-saurs). One of the larger members of this family was the *Deinonychus* (dyne-<u>on</u>-ik-us).

It stood about as tall as a man and had a higher, thicker skull than the *Velociraptor*.

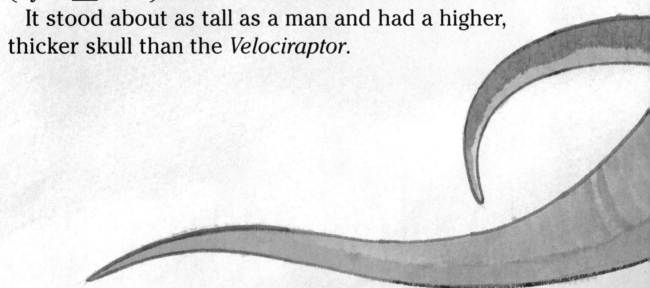

Though much smaller, the *Velociraptor* was related to such gigantic meat eaters as the *Tyrannosaurus rex* and the *Allosaurus*.

Ty-<u>ran</u>-o-saur-us rex

<u>Al</u>-lo-saur-us

The *Velociraptor* had many other, smaller relatives, as well. Of these, the Compsognathus and Gallimimus probably ran very fast. But they may not have been as ferocious as a *Velociraptor*.

Komp-so-<u>nay</u>-thus

Gall-ih-<u>my</u>-mus

O-vee-<u>rap</u>-tor

Ba-ree-<u>ohn</u>-nix

These smaller meat-eaters probably caught insects, small reptiles or the first primitive birds and mammals. One, the *Oviraptor*, may have been a nest-raider, while another, the *Baryonyx*, may have caught fish with its long, curved foreclaws— just like a bear catching a salmon.

The fossil skeleton of a *Velociraptor* was found by scientists in the deserts of Asia.

Fossils of a *Deinonychus* and other raptors were found on the plains of western North America.

The *Velociraptor* and its relatives lived toward the end of the age of dinosaurs—at about the same time as the *Tyrannosaurus rex* and other giant meat-eaters. If a *Velociraptor* had been as big as a *Tyrannosaurus rex*, it would have been a fearsome monster indeed!